NIGHT TOAD

Susan Wicks was born and grew up in Kent and studied French Literature at the Universities of Hull and Sussex. Her first three collections were published by Faber. The first, *Singing Underwater* (1992), won the Aldeburgh Poetry Festival Prize. *Open Diagnosis* (1994) was one of the Poetry Society's New Generation Poets titles. The third, *The Clever Daughter* (1996), was a Poetry Book Society Choice and shortlisted for both T.S. Eliot and Forward Prizes. She has also published two novels and a short memoir, *Driving My Father.* Her latest book is *Night Toad: New & Selected Poems* (Bloodaxe Books, 2003).

She has lived in France, Ireland and the U.S. and held writing residencies in North America and Europe. She currently directs the rapidly growing Writing Programme at the University of Kent.

Susan Wicks

NIGHT TOAD

NEW & SELECTED POEMS

BLOODAXE BOOKS

ISBN: 1 85224 636 7

First published 2003 by
Bloodaxe Books Ltd,
Highgreen,
Tarset,
Northumberland NE48 1RP.

www.bloodaxebooks.com
For further information about Bloodaxe titles
please visit our website or write to
the above address for a catalogue.

Bloodaxe Books Ltd acknowledges
the financial assistance of
Arts Council England, North East.

Cover printing by J. Thomson Colour Printers Ltd, Glasgow.

Printed in Great Britain by
Cromwell Press Ltd, Trowbridge, Wiltshire.

ACKNOWLEDGEMENTS

This book includes Susan Wicks's own selection of poems from her Faber collections *Singing Underwater* (1992), *Open Diagnosis* (1994) and *The Clever Daughter* (1996), together with a new collection, *Night Toad* (2003).

Acknowledgements are due to the editors of the following publications in which some of the new poems first appeared: *Ambit, Critical Quarterly, Cyphers, The Frogmore Papers, The Guardian, The Independent, Leviathan Quarterly, London Review of Books, New Writing 7* (Vintage, 1998), *PN Review, Poetry Ireland Review, Poetry Review, The Rialto, Smith's Knoll, Soundings, Staying Alive: real poems for unreal times* (Bloodaxe Books, 2002), *Thumbscrew*, and *The Times Literary Supplement*.

'Optician' was my response to a short poem commission by the Salisbury Last Words Festival, 1999, and appears in *Last Words* (Picador, 1999). 'Night Toad', 'Wild Bees' and 'Green Hill' were first published in French translation in *Les Annales de la Villa Mont-Noir 98-99.* My own French version of 'Sleeping Alone' has been set to music by Jérôme Lemonnier for Mathilde Mauguière and premièred in Quebec in April 2000. 'Lost' was first broadcast on *The Verb* (BBC Radio 3).

I should also like to thank the Virginia Center for the Creative Arts and the MacDowell Colony, where some of the poems were written, the Brisons Veor Trust on Cape Cornwall and, especially, the Conseil du Nord's Centre départemental de Résidence d'Écrivains européens at the Villa Mont Noir, which gave me both time and the inspiration of its beautiful landscape still scarred by conflict.

Thank you, too, to Edna Zapanta-Manlapaz and the British Council for the Batangas poems and to Simon and Rowena Milner for those based on the tomb of Philip II in Vergina.

CONTENTS

NIGHT TOAD

(2003)

Omens

A click, a gap,
a dead bird on the doorstep,
a cloud shaped like an angel
– and bit by bit
the airwaves swell and fill
with piped laughter; a slug
presses its pale belly to the pane.

A tendril of ivy taps,
a gutter drips. Bees wake,
eat their slow way out between bricks.

And then the walls are down,
every door open and swinging.
Wires snake across the hearth-rug
to the jump and flash
of strobe-light. Where there was moon

a rocket flares. A kiss of lipstick smears
a glass that isn't yours, a stain
unrolls its royal purple in the hall,
there's a pile of strangers' coats
where your bed should be; bodies
lurch and keel over, mouths blink off and on.

Flanders

Estaminet at Ondank Mill

Drink here and you need thank no one –
not the iron frog waiting on its haunches
for the game to start, his maw-pouch frozen open
on a croak that's been forthcoming
a hundred years. Not the barman, whose Flemish greeting
grates in the throat, nor the waitress leaning
her breasts on your dark table
misted with froth. Much less the wind of Flanders
outside, the crust at your eyes' corners,
the sails that strain and shiver
till the bones creak. And least of all
the land itself, the crooked carpenter
who gave this place its name, his work undone,
an airy skeleton, his price
too high, the priest holed in the tower
on a mess of tarnished plate.
                                        This March evening,
greasy with beer and sunset,
the sky moves
in a spreading blur of blood,
leaves the dark earth standing.

The Gift

They gave you nothing,
those young men, frantic, sliding
from duckboards into craters,
drowned by what they carried.

How could they give anything –
their guts churning brown water –
mindless, blank-eyed or gibbering,
even their own names forgotten?

Do you think they could still love
stumps like blackened fingers,
foul gas breaking the surface,
shreds on a barbed tangle?

Your thankyous are relentless:
rank after rank, you keep coming
in French, Flemish, English
as if someone could still hear you,

the land itself waving
its wands of golden willow
over streams bulging with cress
as the little clouds race across.

If they should march back
through this field of green corn –
a face, a pair of boots, a laugh
appearing out of nothing –

you could thank them in person.

Christmas

(from eye-witness accounts of the Great War,
In Flanders Fields Museum, Cloth Hall, Ieper)

Stille Nacht: men's voices rise
from the trenches. In your sights
a man staggers with a fir tree
and you don't shoot –
you watch the small star travel
and come to rest – a stable,
a child bedded in straw
where the warm animals still are.
And men are leaving their watches
for a kick-out in No-Man's-Land,
snipping through wet cotton
with wire-cutters, trading buttons.
Time stops. Time to repair
your cat's-cradle of barbed wire,
bring in your stiffened dead.
You've come so far
with beer, tobacco, oranges:
no wonder you hardly draw breath
there, on the bank at Diksmuide,
feeling the rope vibrate
as the host glides towards you
over the frozen river,
in its rime-bag of cloth.

Het Labyrint

This was a place of lepers.
A bronze boy throws up his hands,
not a finger missing:
leprosy is an old game
of feeling or not feeling.

Inside, the Victorian girls
avert their coy cheeks
all down the stairwell;
a black perambulator hovers
till its baby wakes.

Flattened against the light,
a child's scooter,
its wooden wheels
eaten to stumps.
A gawp of naked dolls.

Hair. A pierced umbilicus
cries *Mama*. Pinball boards
that take me back
to my own childhood.
Jeux de l'oie printed on card

where between the wars
a man is christened, married,
entre à l'hospice
to miss a turn or two.
His line-drawn face.

A huddle of faded Christs
with and without haloes
bless one another
as we drink, nose after nose
baring its white plaster.

Het Labyrint is the name of an estaminet-cum-folk museum
in the village of Kemmel.

Mont des Cats

Up there in every cell
a man wakes, answers the call
to prayer as the echoing voices rise
among wheels of cheese.

Mont Noir

Leconte Marcel, Persin Alfred –
How do I even dare
to enter here, to leave
prints in their soft mud?

To my left, three rows
of crosses – *Henry Eugène* –
from when it began,
the little purple flowers

carefully tended.
And to my right –
Dear loved one, never forgotten –
1918, almost an ending.

April. Eighty-odd years.
A square of green,
the clouds' pewter,
the high bare trees.

Open the metal box
and you discover
we are all visitors:
Brugge, Lille, Poperinge,

Hatfield, Welwyn Garden
City – May it never –
running under rain,
piercing the paper.

German Military Cemetery, Steenwerck

Where ours lie singly, theirs
are two by two, sharing a cross –
two families meet to trample
the same few feet of grass.

They must lie mouth to mouth,
their two deaths fused into one,
each with a single arm
reaching, one south, one north.

Black metal versus white stone,
like something dreamed up,
a problem in a newspaper
crackling in someone's lap.

No flowers, no neat garden,
nothing to prune or plant,
nothing to protect. Just green
played on by shadows that turn

as the dark crosses move on
from blade to blade –
the ghosts of a thousand planes
flying in formation.

I look for a book of signatures
but there's nothing. Here
no one is living: only the dead
tell us exactly who, and where.

Night Toad

You can hardly see him –
his outline, his cold skin
almost a dead leaf,
blotched brown, dull green,
khaki. He sits so quietly
pumping his quick breath
just at the edge of water
between ruts in the path.

And suddenly he is the centre
of a cone of light
falling from the night sky –
ruts running with liquid fire,
cobwebs imprinted on black,
each grass-blade clear
and separate – until the hiss
of human life removes itself,
the air no longer creaks,
the shaking stops
and he can crawl back
to where he came from.

But what *was* this,
if it was not death?

Blockhaus

A small volcanic hiccup
in a sea of field,
the sea itself seasick –
that reeling green
that never rights itself,
and the spring
which can camouflage concrete,
half-drown it in young corn.

Now, in daylight,
its slit mouths gape
like blackened letter slots.
I imagine it
lit from inside,
a concrete pumpkin
flaring against dark.

And here they come, look,
the last stragglers – on bikes,
strung out across the land
like jockeys crouched to the future
in a rainbow of silk.

Wild Bees

At first they come singly, outriders
clinging to a thorn, a blade in my path,
or hovering inches from my cheek,
and then faster, thicker, a dark
whiplash, a moving cylinder of cloud;
the whole sky is black.
There's no way round. I hide my hands,
tighten my small circle of hood,
and go on walking, my eyes sealed shut –
an effigy carved in green wood –
as I tense myself for stings,
listen for flying bodies
to dash themselves against cloth
like rain on canvas – but there's only breath,
a seethe of wings that parts
to let me through, unmarked.
There's not a single bee
caught in my hair or clothes,
though I shake myself. I undo the zip
of my jacket, measure the sunken road
to the hilltop under its murk of cloud.
I sing as I go up.

Border

You can tell you've reached the border
because the cars stop. Under the rain
Sunday couples stroll shoulder to shoulder.

You change into first – you have to pull right out
to avoid a small congregation idling across
as if it could take all night.

No guards, no barriers, no papers passed
from hand to hand. Only this no-man's-land
of bars and toys, this little Las Vegas.

And then you're through, the muddle
of bodies shrinking in glass. There's only you
and a man in black Lycra, punishing the pedals.

Sleepless

Up here is all silence. Then
an owl-call wavers across the hill
as if in warning –
an ending, or a beginning

while night goes on,
interminable, its fingers
parting the trees; pale anemones
flutter under the moon.

And there's some small animal,
a vole or rabbit streaking
into the open, suddenly covered
by a rush of white feathers,

a beak dripping malice.
I begin to see
skin, the fur and frantic claws
an irregular grey bolus

of waste, the delicate skull
impacted, teeth forced shut,
this undigested record
of a life crushed out

and the limbs lifted, twitching
over fields, over a small square
of sleeping graves. 1918.
Even silence is something.

Nothing moves. This place
is the owls'. And he's alone
on lookout, dreaming
of who he loves. I can see his face.

There is a Green Hill

(Mount Kemmel, July 1918)

I have sent my only son
to dance in mud, strip the black willow.

I have heard him call me,
welcomed him on my barbed fingers,

spread the world like a dark map
at his feet, remodelled and slippery.

Here are my words, sent back to me
sweat-ringed, rat-eaten.

The foetus-curve of his body
will never unbend itself.

It has started, the rhythmic music
of dead birds. The sky is full of them.

Between screeches, he can still hear me.
Just testing, I say. *Testing*.

Birds at Dawn

They are taking possession,
their whole transparent world
displacing ours: so many audible voices
to chirp and twitter, the sudden creak
of high wings. And a sharp note like barking –
as if *they* might wake
to hear us calling at the fringes,
similarly strange, through the same dawn,
our songs translating themselves
into mud, into tree-skeletons,
craters where the bodies of birds
lay bleeding. Under its feather shield
a mind drifts, not grasping
what makes the metal sing,
how a man can inhabit
such treeless spaces.

'Chapelle à Locques', Col de Berthen

1

Here is where they end up,
the shreds of our fraying fabric,
the knots and crumpled paper
we kept next to our bodies
as we turned in our beds and sweated,
retched into chipped basins
or fell back, unable to swallow
as the shapes of fruit and flowers
swelled, trapped in our window.

We are rags. The rags smell of us.
They are our stinking prayer.
Pierced, we flap in all weathers,
dead leaves catching on our railings
as pilgrims reach out to finger
our fading threads.

In darkness
we gleam like so many markers
beside the path; the wood empties;
owls call from across the hillside.
A tracker dog, straining at the leash,
could lead his staggering master
straight to us, a whine rising
in his throat, as the pull slackened.

He has found us, he knows the smell
of what we hoped for. His drool
glistens on our shredded stockings.

2

You can see it, the slow procession
of halt and lame – Good Friday
winding its slow way up
through woods to a wedding-cake altar
with pink roses. They circle the chapel,
heads bent under a green shawl
of leaves, renew their intercessions
of torn cloth on painted iron –
child's blue hair-ribbon,
hanky with yellow borders,
balled sports sock grey with weather.
And here he is, prostrate, resting
among purple artificial flowers,
his hair a ripple of plaster,
his long pale legs extended
and flaking, broken-footed.

From his little goatee
you'd think he would be nimble,
escape before they could get to him,
vaulting the iron railings,
leaping from rock to rock.

* * *

Fishing-boat, Aldeburgh

Red roof, bright turquoise hull,
this little fishing-boat puts out to sea
in a confetti of wings. They float up
to scatter themselves again, a fluttering marriage
of sea and sunlight, the boat's live wake.

Against the slate water the white wings glitter
then rise black as crows':

the horizon is too much for them,
too far or too final.

Simple

It isn't necessary to explain it.
The tide has no use for us.
Pebbles lay their subtle greys
on beige whether or not
we name them. Even the sea wall
isn't ours but the sea's.

A wagtail runs on the coping, flies
to perch on a wooden pole
warmed by March sun. I reach out to touch
a bird-pole-shingle-shadow-flick of flight
(now flown).

Fishermen

They camp under black canvas
like men taking pictures
under a cloth. Only their rods jut out
towards the swirl and pucker
of sand, the slow crawl of water.

Almost high tide. They are taking pictures
of time, the time it takes
for a sail to cross the horizon,
for the cries of birds
to become one cry, the smell of salt
to be a smell of earth and trees and vinegar,
for that small fishing-boat
to put out in a flutter of gulls –
for a sudden cataract
to breach that one last spit,
creating a new island.

In warmer waters off Cuba
from a more expensive boat,
Hemingway trolled his fat bait
for giant marlin, under his thumb
a single thread vibrating
to the tune of live muscle. Scattering water,
the fish jumps,
throws the bloodied hook
and the man's left suddenly alone
in slack harness
with a length of dead line.

I wasn't patient enough.
Not a strong enough swimmer.
Is that what they mutter
from their black hides
as they watch the rod's shadow
turn towards the summer?

Room Service

The staff at this hotel are chosen
for their beauty. They come and go
discreetly with their airborne trays
of sweating glasses, peanuts, San Miguel
while the pianist dreams over the keys,
half-closing his almond eyes.

Out there, beyond the orchids,
pineapples, papayas, palms fan out
their fingers on the night glass
like starving children. Nine floors up
across my bed a terry robe extends
flat arms, a complimentary caress.

I'll whisper my strangled bidding –
omelette, asparagus – and when he comes
I'll tip too much. Next night I'll find the phone
within arm's reach, the menu open
on my pillow, think of his perfect lips
politely shaping, *You are alone?*

Coral

I came down for this,
to hang flat as a shadow
over their subtle landscape,

their ferns of coral parting
to let me in, my thighs
grazing their mock fungus.

When they see me, they scatter
like hail or seed,
changing direction quickly,

their little panic glinting
bright blue. A black angel
trails its shred of fin.

They swim round and under me,
lead me to deeper places,
starfish joined like blue fingers.

I can crush thousands
of soft bodies, close my hand,
snap off their brittle histories.

The blackened antlers pierce me
through my soles
as blood leeches out of me,

leaves its rusty smoke
across their sky.
They know where to find me.

Sliding Windows

The eye moves down
from coco-thatch,
through paper sky,
brushwork of leaves,
the sea a gleam
between the characters
of crippled trunks,
to spilt magenta
petals on wet stones.
Above, the fan's
flicker of blades
circles the day
from fighting-cock
to child crying
and the page stirs:
a wave begins
to swell, aromas
breathe, lean
towards water
as a fattened drop
plummets from thatch
to palm-leaf,
making it shiver.
Tomorrow
an uncut chapter.

From a Hammock Between Aroma Trees

Lie back and the air holds you
strung between shore and tideline,
your head towards the mountain,
your feet going before you
to the island. You rock unseen;
aromas spread their green feathers
over your woven boat. No sudden light,
no leaving, only the steady gleam
of sky on water. This is your body,
this the space it swings in. Look,
the sun rolls between your bare toes
like an orange. A firefly's spark.

Sleeping Alone

Tonight will be my first night,
the air entering as it pleases,
leaving me porous, and wiser.

Tonight I shall watch the moon
cast its sliding shadow
on my sheets, in the pit of my pillow.

Rolled in my mouth, my tongue
is growing fat. By morning
it will have found the farthest places.

I will be silver, I will be slippery,
turning under fine meshes
till the fisherman throws up his hands

and runs from me. I will be solitary.
Even dreams will abandon me,
the sea wind translate

whatever it can stir of me,
my feet entering the morning
while my head still sleeps,

the distant shoreline receding
and irrelevant, its line of strung flesh
already salted, drying.

Waves curl from me across coral
long and light as bones
that break and belong to no one.

I will stretch out my limbs
to the bed's unwrinkled corners
and touch nothing. When I wake

no one will have known me.

The Art of Half-Sleeping

This house is taking flight,
its roof of palm-thatch rising
from the hill, its windows of shell
like open wings. Below me, waves crinkle,
falling between my bare toes.

My heartbeat becomes the slap
of outriggers on water
as a boat slides its dark finger
across the bay and the fan's blades
whirl into stillness. Somewhere nearby

a fighting-cock lets rip,
makes morning of 6 p.m., yet the panes
admit no image – only the sky's dying
flame through milk, a bloodshot
cataract of light.

When I next see my father
and he asks me, *How is your father?*
I shall say he is well and half-sleeping
in a house thatched with coconut,
his red sun sinking through capiz.

Good Person

The gods are weighing us, me
and my father. We sit on our twin pans and look
forwards into nothing, trying
to stay upright. He is
the heavier. They do this for our sake.

He has learned not to be wasteful.
He keeps crumbs.
He has been saving himself
in small pieces. Eyes front, he goes down
sedately. Surely they mean us no harm.

They incline their good faces – the very same
as in that childhood playground when I ran
to the seesaw, mounted, flew for a moment, and then
nothing, someone else sinking
through my skin, someone's blood on the beam.

Rooting for Pikachu

Your world has shrunk to this –
a view of rubbish bins and grass,
a rhododendron bush. Inside, bare walls
still wait for pictures. Only the TV
spatters your afternoon with life-size
dayglo animals. You lie and doze,
a matchstick foetus, while a cartoon crashes
Pokemon blue. *Uh-uh*, says Pikachu,
shaking his floppy ears. He won't transmute
to giant Raichu: if he's got to die
he'll die like this. I hold your plastic cup
but swallowing's too hard, as if you've made a vow
to shrink to nothing, to a crumpled ball
of bone and breath. The giant mouse
is raising his fat fist. I try to ease my hand
from yours but can't release
your child-grip on my finger –
you can't let go.
And Pikachu stands blinking, with his little face
all patched with plaster crosses.

Miles from here, in high-rise flats and houses
kids lean forward on their couches,
hug their knees and whisper
Pikachu, we love you,
you're so brave, oh, you can beat him, please
don't leave us. Tears
run down their cheeks in wavy rivers.

Birds over Tonbridge High Street

From our cars
we watch them ride the air, their wheeling shape
escaping and reforming, bunched opaque
and thinned, their angled wings
transparent as they turn, suddenly
letting the light through. I squint,
trying to track them. But each single bird
is nothing, flies with the flock and turns
and flies again until it goes to roost
in a tight fist. Another hour
and I'll be at your bedside. By the chart
they wash you, turn you, while you grow
transparent, as the days
bring other deaths – a fall from a flight of steps,
a car exploding, mobile phones
thrown from a crumpled train. The dark ellipse
unskeins itself, remasses, pulses
its black heart, disperses,
fades to a shred
of smoke, comes back
a rippling flag of birds,
a dancing flock.

Clutch

You used to tell me it was like two plates
touching, rubbing together. You'd raise your hands
and I would see two Sunday dinners –
roast potatoes, gravy, Brussels, steaming meat –
heaped up from week to week, always the same meal.

These days your hands won't open, clenched
on cotton wool. By Detling Hill
I'm down to 30, 20, crawling. A few more miles
and this old car of yours is for the hard shoulder.
Its engine whirrs. The two hands meet and part,
transmitting impotence, the plates red-hot.

Charity Christmas Cards

Among the Help the Aged a metallic tree
of Zimmer frames and tripods on a ground
of parchment; snow with snowman; three
small penguins skating on a congealed pond.

Arthritis has a seasonal display
of Christmas roses, holly, swollen knees
like ripe discoloured fruit. The tight bouquet
is framed with gold, the bowl Chinese.

But Parkinsons has got the meaning best –
Mary with all the trimmings – donkey, angels, straw –
in a stained-glass circle: by a bizarre twist
Joseph has become the son-in-law

while almost naked, gurgling on his bed,
the little father lies encased in lead.

Seasickness

(after a misericord in St David's Cathedral – to my father)

We are the wooden people –
the saint leaning to vomit, the hatted man,
the eyeless woman frozen in the stern.
The wave cups us
like God's hand.

The seat-ledge is our roof.
Under its canopy we float
on a still swell. After a while
we'll stretch and take our bearings – land
will come to us, we'll finish
retching our guts out.

And you're the sleepy one
sunk in the bows, half-smiling,
your oar piercing the boat's flank,
your ten fingers spread
across the wood, as if about to play

the brown song of nausea,
the last song before rescue,
a riff to the night sky.

London

There are miles to go and he'll walk them
without legs, leaving his bones behind him.
His money's in the bank. His smile sleeps in pink plastic.
There's nothing to stay for. The window's wide open.

He'll tie the morphine patches
in a bundle of spotted hanky,
sling them over his shoulder, turning
and turning again, whatever the bells tell him.

Z

What my father needed was a z-shaped coffin
slash – slash – slash

But undertakers must have special scissors
snip – snip
to cut the tightened tendons behind a client's dead knees

Now he is with God
in heaven in the arms of my mother
Crunch

I loved him
as much as anyone *can* love a letter

And none of us is truly coffin-shaped
Slash – snip – crunch – howl – clatter

Taking Off

In dreams he's learning to walk again.
His little Chinese shuffle
plays shufti with the Zimmer till the metal bars gape open
to let him through. He raises his stick and twirls it,
knocks blossom from high branches. The straw hat shimmies
in a blur of moving fingers as he croons *Ebb Tide* and exits
backwards. Only last night
he bounded up a flight of steps, a pyramid, a whole mountain.
Not long and he'll be running
for the 9.05, he'll dance a fox-trot, swim
as he never could in life. He'll take off.

Soon he'll be crouching in wartime planes again. The moonlit earth
will ripple under him like rucked cloth.
He'll lean to whisper, *Darling*. And, *Forget this dying lark.*
Behind the airman's shades his eyes will open,
as the pilot brings her round again into the wind.
They'll buzz the officers' mess and rise, laughing.

The Day of Your Father's Funeral

(Farncombe/Mont Noir, September 1997 – for J.H.)

It was a humanist funeral, you told me, chosen
because of belief, or the lack of it, the day golden,
end of September *while to speeches and feasting*
the players rode in on their gleaming engine;

the readings appropriate, taken from a large library
of inspiring words, *as with a wrist-flick*
the juggler sent the white ball spinning
and the glass tipped backwards. The bare-chested showman

spewed fire into the trees. Your son read something,
the verses suddenly blurring
as you held your daughter, *while in the corner*
of our eye the white-feathered creatures

danced gravely on stilts, dipping their graceful
horns and beaks, his face a boy's, his story ending
as it was meant to, full circle, gently
as rain fell from overhead, the sky cloudless.

Lost

It will begin with a forgetting of names –
the man next door, the town, the street you live in.
You'll be found wandering in woodland.

Small objects will be misplaced –
keys in a vase, a holed sock in the fridge,
a coat-hanger under your pillow.

The woman who sells vegetables
will be Your Majesty. All paths
are rabbit-paths, narrow and twisting.

Money becomes inscrutable, the coinage indistinct,
heavy with hidden meaning. The notes ripple;
lines converge in a star of branches.

You're lost, wearing your green dress.
You answer the phone before it rings
and a voice says, *birch, ash, green willow.*

Scratch

I shall live out my life in soft cotton,
my flaking skin innocent
of the spaced red welts of buttons.

In the narrow mornings
I'll lie hardly breathing
on glass, watching the street turn milky.

Towards lunchtime I shall possibly
put on my quilted gown, its silk tassels
dangling, slithery as fishes.

I will keep watch on my hands,
muffle my fingers' itch
in summer gloves. Nothing will touch me

but a slick of unguents
in labelled jars delivered to my door.
At the prescribed hour

my good husband will anoint me,
turn from me in a rasp of blanket,
his mouth falling open.

All night I'll scratch
while blood sings in my broken skin
like salt, until death comes to me.

The Lighthouse-keeper

I am not here, they say. I'm obsolete,
the last of a line of dead,
my life untenanted.
Where I squint towards land
a perfect eye goes round and round.
The things I've seen and felt
are manufactured now. Where I once slept,
the hiss of blowing sand,
a glass crusted with salt.
Yet I've seen cold
in all its colours, beds of weed
a heave of dark bubbles, floating
as the world lurches,
reaches white arms to clap
a passing ship. A falcon
blown from Greenland turns its ruffled head
wondering how it got here,
cut off from its kind.
The shoreline twinkles. On a clear day
I can see bathers, walkers, twitchers
with their apparatus trained
on my lump of rock. And once, a bee,
till it died of hunger, buzzed
in smaller and smaller circles and gave up
its puzzled ghost.
The sun's silver shadow gleams
like a shoal of white fish.
Sometimes I see nothing.
The mist sends back to me
my eye's own white
like a yolkless egg.
Sometimes I run to earth
down my own white needle,
reeling, hearing the gulls laugh.

I miss the language: from my buzzing box,
nothing but French or Spanish,
Roscoff or Santander. There's no one here
for me to pound with words

or whisper to up close as the sea does.
No birdsong shaping the small trees
behind my eyes, no fields of daffodils
or wind-farms' frantic turning on the hill,
no semaphore of blades.
I miss the streams, their bed-sweat smell
of flowering garlic, the donkey that came to my hands
in the hope of something, the barmaid's grooved back
as she filled my glass, and overhead
the optics glinting. I miss even the wrecks,
a drunken carcass spewing across rocks
and the slick of dark blood floating,
turning each fish and bird
to a blackened statue. What's a wife
but the pull and suck of water at high tide
in a rip of lace? One night the shore was wet
with dying jellyfish. My sweeping light
made mucus of them all. I picked them off
and threw them over, watched them drift
out of my beam's reach
till each last cleft was empty, scoured clean.

I have a picture of her face
taken at Mên-an-tol, in a frame of granite.
Each time I look at it she seems to age.
Those are her mineshaft eyes
that stare from the cliff
to where at dusk sometimes the blue islands
rise out of nothing. I hung a lock of her hair
beside my door like seaweed to fatten on spray
or splinter like spaghetti in my palm
till the wind wore it to ravels, to a shred
of sheep's wool caught on a wire.
I felt and the nail was bare.
Since then the boats come in
without my help. My severed beam
bloodies the clifftop houses one by one,
reddens the shuttered windows,
conjures a shock of flame
from a gorsebush, and moves on.
I trust that no one's died
– or only that little death –

the breathless crowd
last summer, on the beaches, bodies entwined
for the moment of truth –
a frisbee of dark silence
flicked from horizon to horizon
as the birds stopped singing.
Mine was the automated gleam
that pierced it for a moment, searching, unmanned.

Since I became redundant I sweat fish,
pick crystals of salt
from my nostrils, poke my thumb
through a wall of shining water.
Sometimes at low tide
I crouch at the waves' edge
and shit in the bladder-wrack,
one brown bubble more,
a warm Medusa, something of my own
for them to know me by.
My innards dissolve.
If they should radio me now
in a crackle of fusing tongues
I'd turn them off.
If a boat arrived
laden with Christmas cheer
I'd send it packing.
This blind world is mine.
Now Boat and Priest are blotted out
there's only the light. My skin
is a web of sores, my hands are papered bone,
but I'm still here. I wake and keep it turning
under its flat hat
like a pastor, indistinguishable from a machine.

Boat Cove and Priest's Cove are the two small beaches on
either side of Cape Cornwall.

Like This

Squat, squashed into herself, the woman in my mirror
is not quite right. Is it her face? Something in the colour
of her clothes? He says, *Bend forwards*, and she squirms, slumps
in her chair. *Could you tilt your head this way?* She goes limp.

A gentle pressure on the nape, the scissors' quick snip
as the black crescents fall, coaxed from the comb. In her lap
they must accumulate, they must be making stars
or snowflakes, a black drift invisible in the glass.

Is this how you part it? A white path runs from the crown
and is lost, buried in bushy growth. The young man
smiles and interprets. *Like this? Like this.* The skilful blades
play over her scalp – till she sees her new self and explodes

into laughter, raucous, improbable. *Now, can we settle down?*
His voice resigned. I turn and see her hunched, gowned,
in a ring of black feathers. She can't fight it, the great joke
that racks her. And we laugh with her, till our sides ache.

Contact

She is writing to a young prisoner
on Death Row. She imagines him
in the South – a truant childhood
under scraggy trees, a breaker's yard
of battered parts where wings
and fenders lie scattered, rusting
under green. How can she hope to know him:
the colour of his speech, his letters bulging
with mis-spelt words, his words a river
where the stripped bodies turn over
like dark logs? In letters he escapes towards her,
shooting the night's rapids
to where she lies, the English moonlight
pooling under her ribs. She is shaking
as she reads it: his words have found her
sleepless under the eaves, the glass of her window
flowing to earth, its brittle journey
older than he imagines, older
than he is ever likely now
to imagine. In her dreams she turns over
his last few words, the way he makes her
skin jump, her husband and children tossed aside
like junk. She must be
some kind of murderer
or she would not be here, would not
be watching for news, for the one morning –
sun in her lashes, footfalls,
those first 2,000 volts. Contact. A body changing
its colour. The one-way mirror.

Breaking the Waves

She would give you everything –
the smile crossing her face
like wind on water,
the God she throws her voice to,
but deeper.

Her last few pennies
dropped in the public slot,
the glass box ringing and ringing.

The man in the country bus,
his rank prick flapping between her fingers,
the children who trail and stone her
like a dog; the sailor,
his nifty blade
carving her to a totem.

She gives you sand
trickling from a sealed coffin,
her voice a bell sounding across water.

What would you give her?
Your thoughts? Your life for hers?
Her freedom?
God's lewd whisper?

Incident on the M25

The man at the wheel is remaking
my future. It is fiction. I am unable
to believe in it. And yet he comes closer,
he is pushing his dark weight
across my path, his painted sides
almost lean in, the two of us suspended
in held breath, our two engines purring together,
our ill-matched bodies
parallel – though I am already
touching the brake, almost
edging away from him.
We meet. He leans on me
with his cold freight as chrome
twists and snaps between us. A crash
and we lock, veering
towards the fast lane. Then he swings free,
oblivious, filling my whole screen.
And I replay it: how I must already
have been invisible, how the frame of his mirror
held only sky. Now my near flank
tells its own story – gashed and streaked
with blue, the mirror-lane behind me
swept away. As I drive home
the flakes of glass fall in, shining,
not quite innocent, not quite
like anything I have encountered.

Duchess of Malfi

(for Bridget)

You are the one clear thing
in a world of purple
coils of bent wire and pillars,
eyes that glitter
under the lights. You enter
through a lace of gates,
touch your burning taper
to the candles, to a flame
that flickers out so fast –
you're taking a husband,
gorging on apricots –
now three growing children,
barely half an hour to separate
the first birth from the last.
You bid them farewell
as if you had lived already,
understood the ending –
three shadow-corpses swinging
on gauze, the rant and slaver
of madmen. *Let them come in.*
And then the loop of rope
on your own pale neck, the crack
as it tightens.
                                        So you are
put out, the gleaming dress
is laid to rest. Two hours
from unripe fruit
to old rope. Now we wait
for the flat dark
when you can stand and leave
unseen – the rope, the candlestick,
the chalice gathered up,
the wrought gates gaping open
on their silent hinges.

Statues

They stand here in a shocked silence,
these grouped bodies in cold dresses,
their eyes downcast; the hands quietly gesture
from this flaking grotto of wishes.

But something flares in a corner –
gladioli, tongues spurting into darkness:
someone has been here before us.

Is it food these people are asking for
or freedom? We wrench the heavy door open
on a flat world, an ordinary crossroads,
silos swaying in a hot ripple.

This is not the chapel
we were looking for, these are not
gods we ever worshipped. We walk out into a rising
hot breath, the give of our tarry footprints.

Église Monolithe, Aubeterre

Who were they, this race of strewn bone?
Did they have hair and skin?
Did they stand at the mouth and watch
for birds, for the spring coming?

A pelvis, a knee-cap. Were they one man
or separate in flesh, brother
and brother? Did one refuse food
while the other hoed his steep garden?

Did they share this cold vision:
a hard tide, wind and waves arrested,
white horses of pocked stone?
When death came, did they join hands?

And what of the far wall, its hewn cross
the height and breadth of a man,
or the font-cross, rough-hollowed
for a child to hide in and never be found?

The shadows bloat. My eyes play tricks
with dark. The stone chambers protrude –
death in bas-relief: a hood, a warm cheek
smelling of garlic, a trailing hem.

In the small skulls the sockets bulge.
Which of them were monks, and which
were here almost from the beginning?
The light inhabits them, its memory of flame.

Hawk, Trees, Earth

It is the same shiver:
the hawk's wings as he hangs
over his prey, the young poplars
in the valley, warm air
rising from earth.

The earth
steadies the tree's roots;
the tree reaches
to guide the hawk home; the hawk
stills the horizon with his eye.

Or the hawk wheels
to the shaking tree, the tree
litters the rough earth
with flakes of shade, the shadows
run, streaking like small animals.

Cones, Chantérac

They were a pair.
I picked them up
in the woods, from between
the barbed hair
of brambles, the rearing heads
of fern, the green

rush of growth.
They were enormous,
each scale distinct, the stems
exposed – bigger than both
my fists, two hundred nipples
like dull gems.

Out in the damp,
this one has closed,
to a half-sized, bland
tessellated lump –
tiles or wooden patchwork
in my open hand.

Yet even now
it shakes, it is stirring
its rings of shadow: cracks
open on a slow
spiral of darkness:
the tiered bracts

reach from the heart
as it expands to admit light.

You can't tell them apart.

Optician

His pencil of light
draws me the bare branches
of my eye's blood,
sap rising in darkness
deep under the lid.

A frieze of trees repeating
on my wall of red –
the shades I lost,
painted by touch,
blaze under his torch.

Now the light is out
but the lines wait –
my deer and bison running
in their red cave.
The fire they outlive.

Rape of Persephone, Vergina

She frowns. This rape is serious.
She's not yielding to anyone.
The red of her streaming hair
has left its rusty thumbprint
as she lies across him, wooden.

His hair's as wild as hers
and the same colour. He stares into the future
and sees no staging-post,
only this long road shrinking
into dust, where his hand lies painted
on her breast and nothing
will wash her from his flesh.

He whips up his tired horses.

Walkman

Watching this old guy cycling
to his own stately rhythm
in anorak and sunglasses,
the yellow flex gyrating
as he pedals, wobbles round corners,
I'm reminded of my father,
the white noise battering his eardrums
as he wailed his broken music
and went on without my mother.
He judders silently onwards
by the rusting hulls of dredgers,
reaches the white tower
and turns inland, continues
his rickety way northwards
past flower-shops and kiosks,
over cool, watered pavements
in a haze of morning blue
to Theodorakis, Zorba, bouzoukis.

Find

The pyre I have built for you contains many animals
caught in a splash of sun under leafy branches.
I have pressed my two thumbs to their warm windpipes
and squeezed gently till the legs crumpled.
I have walked backwards, dragging them over the earth
as their bodies swept us a clean path.
I have brought branches. I have brought oil and kindling,
lifted the heavy jug till a transparent curtain
hung from the lip. I have brought silver, turquoise,
gold. I have brought myself,
my heavy hair, my rituals of mourning, my barbarian languages
and lain two thousand years, trapped in expensive metal
under their feet. Now they discover us, incredulous.
Their maps pinpoint us, their spades expose us,
bring us to light in a red lake
of blowing poppies. The hills ring to their competing voices.

Unnamed

After the body cooled
in the ashes on the high platform
they gathered the bones and washed them
in wine, wrapped them in embroidered purple.
They laid them with the gold wreath,
the wafer-thin leaves and acorns,
in a casket with a last starburst
in its lid, the points of his dead compass.
And in the farthest corner
the unknown woman lay buried
at his feet. Who was she? Cleopatra?
One of his latest wives? She was
wrapped in purple, mid-twenties,
nameless, a grey-white jumble
of femur and metatarsal
and rib. I think she was his daughter,
that she washed her own bones in something
stronger than wine. I think she
stitched her own cloth and saw it
rot into lace, wove her metallic crown
of myrtle and crushed the berries,
wrote her name over and over
on papyrus before she ate it.
She was the one who built
the pyre with its sifted treasure
of turquoise and white clay horses
that leapt from the flames, an explosion
of muscle and hoof and fetlock. She was
the one who prepared the banquet,
who lifted the oil and poured it,
who herded and killed the animals –
who called herself she-goat, chicken,
the innards still warm and steaming
as his no longer did, her heart pounding
with grief, as the ground opened
and blood ran crooked to her elbow.

The Morning After

Grey light, and the animals
have gone, a slur of footprints.
The world creaks. Rotten tree-trunks
lie down on a bed of splinters
to be covered, and Mary
is pie-eyed, yawning, the blue folds
hiding the ragged places
of new blood, as Joseph scrubs at
his hands. Angels
have become ordinary,
a matter of straw and torchlight.
Now the stars
have shrunk back into the grey.

The parents listen
for their child's breath,
not quite believing
he is real, this perfect flesh
is real and can be satisfied
with simple milk, not quite believing
him born into a time
of census and grey footprints
where their own lives continue.

Woodstove

This is an ordinary woodstove –
of long vintage, admittedly –
smoky, cantankerous. Not easy,
he told me, the old glass
scribbled in a black pattern
that does not resemble words,
sparks bursting with a snap
as the fine kindling catches,
the red flames combed forwards,
boiling across the brick ceiling
like a small firestorm. Not
like a firestorm, these logs crumbling
to a city of charred bodies
somewhere in Germany, sometime
before I was born, these iron walls
ticking. No city,
no bodies, and the orange glass
not amber. When I leave
the red heart is still visible,
the hot blood
barely flowing. But in the morning
as I rake the dead embers
the scent of pine and birch
lingers, the cold lip greets me
with its fresh snowfall of ashes.

No Brother

I am thinking of Seymour, his austere messages
under starlight. I am thinking of Franny
prostrate on that sofa, her glossy parting
flattened by too much knowledge; of Zooey,
the endless cigarette glowing,
the foam on his lip.
                                        Here I am
out of my life. The white pines
reach up into sky, the bare deciduous crowns
of silver birches, their giant shadows
cutting a swathe of light on the path,
                    a promise of faces
flattened at my screen-door, grid of fine wire
blown to a blur, fingers rattling the casing,
blood on the page.
                                    I think of Seymour
lying down near the shore-line, his blanket, the bullet
entering his temple, I comb that limpid water
for clues.
                When I call home
my husband tells me nothing
has happened in my life; my daughter tells me
Salinger had no brother.

One White

We are unlearning vision. Under rain the snow
rises into mist, the earth itself is lighter.
Pale clods shrink back, part to show
a bowl of dark leaves, the sudden fruit of water.

Mist ghosts the high trees, their ragged
rigging of needles. A barn
drifts into focus like the barns of childhood
rising through dusk and gone.

Let them go. Let this one wreck
shake off its rags, single
and forgettable, this one shade of white

spread between air and earth. No sight
to speak of. Only the cornea's tingle,
the rank smell of the brook.

The Snow-life of Trees

A sudden gust, and I am invisible,
swirled in a fog of crystals,

cloud-powder, snow rising through sunlight
like smoke. As it slides from them

their lightened limbs drift upwards
into sky, waving. Tomorrow

they will be heavy again, their needles
oblique with snow, awaiting

each silent detonation.
Under them my boots flounder,

my own limbs flex and straighten
as if I were used to walking

in a white explosion of ice
that chokes me on the path and holds me

blinded, a captive – releases me
to stumble under pines, rootless

and merely human, no relation.

Setback

A setback, darling. Death
will be like this: bare trees
through glass, a streaky sunrise
like any other, the earth
whitish. Words leave, leak
from me like urine, my palate
spongey to the tongue as I wait
for a buzz of nurses. I'm snoring awake.

Just – somewhere – something – this bird,
that twig. *Nothing to get upset about.* My mother's
soft voice or my daughter's, half heard
as the world floods back. Feathers
flick at the window, flame-coloured, and the branch
bounces on air, the bird gone. A finch.

Points North

My early morning sleep is a map
spread under migrating geese. Through dreams
I hear them, their torn skeins pulled taut
as the horizon recedes, as the hills flatten
to wing-flap and heart-beat, their raucous
repetitious honk in startled blue
like someone gasping for breath. Through eyelids,
the drawn white of curtains,
I sense sunlight vibrating, this March morning
cool and traversable, the sudden mirrors
of lakes. And I imagine them
changed by this overwintering, ragged,
their struck reflections leaving
pink vapour-trails of blood, that last shadow
floundering and struggling to keep up,
the yards of clear air
unbridgeable. Harsher and more intimate
than sleep, their voices come to me
from the south: imagined half-life;
migration. Forgive me.
A wing dips to evening, the deep black
bones of waiting trees. I see us
teased out over creaking pines,
ragged, reforming
in a perfect arrow-head; I hear us
as we fly north to try the ripe ice
of Canada, flapping, honking like crazy.

FROM

THE CLEVER DAUGHTER

(1996)

Rain Dance

This is how they make rain, the raw
repeated drumbeat of two pulses, this green gauze
that settles on their skin and gleams
like light on water. This is how he creates her,
fluid as green drops fusing
on new growth, bent to this holy posture
of damage, her raised green satin instep
stroking her own right cheek, as he still turns her,
twists her as if through creepers,
this green sediment of branches
layered on air, as his taut body
dances on hers. They will reach the light soon. He bends her
this way and that, her head flips backwards
into his darkness, her neck surely broken.
Her two legs split perfectly open
like roots. There is moisture
between them now as he drags her, wood
rasping her inside thighs. The rapt watchers
gasp with her pain, if she could only
feel it. Curved for his blessing,
her skin glistens as he still strokes her
like a green pot into being
on this wheel of rhythms
where they are gods, unmindful now of bodies,
our single-jointed history
of breakage, and the sweat runs off them.

Human Geometry

The soft line of her arm
extends under the table, her hand touches

his knee. Somewhere outside perception
the planes of their two bodies

come together. Later in warm darkness
I represent them, their two forms congruent

under stars, their eyes closed, speaking
no shared language. I hear them,

the hiss of their late-night shower
on the tiled wall, their urine

running in the bowl, her precise footsteps.
I trace her conjectural return

to a segment of shared circle
labelled with letters, her chord of voices

rising like children's, the arc of his body
melting on hers like a solution.

Room of His Own

You can tell his wife has left him, from books
and letters that slide on each surface, the paper
in the shower shredding to mildew, the stark
pupating clothes-line, folded for winter.

These are her dust-motes floating over a chair
to suck up sun, her framed daughter
caught in a net of light, her fine hair
lifted on deep grass from another era.

What he has is a view over trees, a few things
that are his, a drift of bills in the hall
to trip him as he turns his recalcitrant key

in the lock: this long room where he can be
himself, his posters curled on the wall,
shirts clinging to banisters like damp wings.

My Daughter at Kilpeck

Beyond this small church, my daughter
stands on a green lip, her back
straight and still, her hair lifted
against corn-stubble, the grey uncertain
weather of late summer. Slowly I circle
one last time, look up to study
the stuck corbels – boar, ram, lion,
dog and rabbit – their eyes still watching
for the stone huntsman, as above me his woman,
cold clinch of knees and elbows,
yanks her stone slit open
as if for blood. I slip back into the dark
between carved folds, and see my daughter
still in the same green place
while over us the sharp creature
face erodes, a slow strand of hillside
probes her like moist silk
and moves on, through her stone lips
into harvest, the eye of her needle.

Landing

We meet on landings: outside the night
is furred with frost. You are warm,
sleepy as fruit, your peach satin
pyjamas rumpled, scented with breath.

Below us an old house
hums. Through windows the dark
is a net of trees, trapped stars.
Darling, in the cold airways

a woman flares in a reek of petrol,
children murder children with bricks. Bodies
such as yours lie buckled, blackened
on hard shoulders. Sleepless,

I meet you, we cling to each other,
our hearts beat back gravity, feathered
in red juice like a split stone.

Fox

The evening my mother died we first saw
its face – fur, a moment's meeting
of eyes, a quick ripple from the path
into undergrowth. Over us, the green reaching
of birch and beech, the new tangle
of wild honeysuckle. And repeating,
that one cuckoo, its measured heartbeat
across grass and bluebells. Then a second time,
rounding a blind bend, the brush lifted
on a ground of sunlight, seeming to give us
darkness, the spine seeming to open
a new space hidden between tree-trunks,
the gap that would let it slip to earth again,
the tight bracken masking it over.

Understairs

This is where you would hide
from your own mother
as she screamed and ranted
till they came to take her:
cobwebs across faces,
gas-pipes, inscrutable pointers,
the old mop with its grey head
leaning. Knotted rags
hang by the half-closed
boxes of turning apples.
On a ripple of dust and cider
your empty wicker basket
rocks undiscovered. Daughters,
we huddle together, hands
to our mouths, stopping
the high voices.

Persephone

Wanting someone who looked natural,
they cast you as Persephone, not thinking
how at regular intervals you were taken
to visit your own mother
under a flaking sky of cream paint
down the echoing corridor
to the long-stay ward, where trees
froze in the black glass
of winter – how you were no stranger
to the clockwork rhythms of figures
moaning and swaying, the mechanical
hands that moved across faces
or scattered things in odd corners,
the hungry hands that flapped after
with their wings of ragged knitting.
Each time you would leave her and return
to birdsong, the urgent green
through frost, the melting grass, the world
you would give her if she would only
recognise you through the heavy doors
your father closed between you. Each week
you rehearsed your flower-steps
with a basket of paper petals
as your teachers smiled down on you, exclaiming
at your sweet face,
at the way you seemed never to see him coming –
as if each last dance were the first dance,
and every mother won over by so little.

Grandmother

These were my mother's: against a window
of trees, sky, sunlight, I fill sacks
with intimate things, tear up, pull down,
straighten my aching back. Here are
the home-made pyjama trousers
with no jackets, the wilting knickers,
the corset she bought and could never quite
squeeze herself into. Her old soft
working-dresses cling to me. Here is
the long escaping coil of child's hair
in its hood of crumpled paper, the letter
about the French kissing, the photograph
of myself at eight, eyes clear and
watchful, the little covered basket
of soaps, the handkerchiefs embroidered
in foreign countries. And in a dark box
where the painted birds flutter,
my father's one last tooth, yellowed,
long as a wild animal's, gleaming
between the frayed silk scarves,
the lacy night-things of a grandmother.

Flames

This is the black and white photograph
that I shall burn first, my young mother
in the wind at Margate,
self-conscious and smiling as the child
pulls back and away from her
and sulks, the silver-paper glitter of kite-tail
still streaming. These are the
flames, the crackling red and orange,
the hungry black ring that moves outwards.
And this one, with my father
standing on a mound to reach up
another two inches, as she looks laughing
over canal, trees, valley, the Dijon summer
colours disappearing in a stroke
of rising light, the transparent centre.
Or this one, taken much later,
the two of you always together,
against bulb-fields blazing
with red tulips, that I shall
leave until last, that perhaps I will not need
even to put a match to.

Bubbles

A microwave has replaced my mother.
We divide its clear wrapping between us
with scissors, letting our fingers travel
over the fat blisters, remembering
the bladder-wrack of our lost summers,
a slippery harvest of rank gases.

Climbing the stairs I hear it
rising at our heels, the frantic crackle
of four bare soles as my daughters
dance on air, the multiple small explosion
of crushed cells from Atlantis.

Buried in her things I found a picture
of bubbles, drawn in my childhood,
the bright circles crowding up to heaven
with primitive passion, my own
oh dear one's poped, trying
to describe departure.

Listen with Mother

Only this: an old armchair,
a sideboard, sun on carpet;
time, and the child
uncurls, strokes the warm
dog sleeping, dances
to find her mother. She can
hear her, the sweet small
chink of glass in the kitchen,
a tap running. No need
to listen, she will always
dance from the chair,
the old dog will always
be sleeping. On tiptoe
she is skipping
across carpet towards her
busy music of absence, the
clash of crockery, the cold tap's
gurgle rising and falling.

Blind Date

Among the tables and steel teapots
I thought I was meeting a stranger.

A pot of tea for us, a miracle,
your hand raising and raising it.

The same rain on our two faces
as we talk of the same lost lover.

Now that you are dead, I find
our two griefs are compatible.

Dispersal

My mother is dispersed. The open window
admits her body.

The soapy water turns, retains the shape
of her rough finger;

the steam from the runner beans displaces her
only slightly.

I fill my lungs with her, hold, expel her gently
into sunlight.

The grass under the apple tree pushes up into her.
A creeping wasp

buries itself deep in her dark places.

On Re-recording Mozart

When the throb of her voice was cut off, I drove
through streets white with silence: no sound
but my own engine, as if above or beyond
the gear-change a knife glittered, and love

itself were cut out, its high vibrating tongue
docked with a neat flick as the full reel
still turned, clicking, lashing its little tail
at nothing, and silence became her whole song.

Now I have re-recorded Mozart, my tape
unwinding across chasms. Between one note
and the next she still breathes. Her breath

pulls me across darkness, the last escape
of bodies. Rising from her new throat
it redeems and redeems us. I have erased death.

Mute Swans

In the still evening two swans,
twin ghosts across black water,
glide closer and the two beaks
merge, the stretched pale necks fuse
to a perfect heart, squeezed ever tighter
until the dark centre
fills, the last gleaming feather
dies in the curve of the bodies'
slow shrinkage to a half-remembered
mouth, a hat, a white bow floating
on deep water.

But no, they have
passed each other, they separate,
they have vacated the night's mirror,
that last light from the sky,
the symmetry
that made disappearance necessary.

Weir

You died long ago and the trees
in the river are thin copper
beaten to sunlight. In moving water
our world is precious as wreckage,
its sunken carcass rolled and
remade; the impact of a drop
rings us like deep treasure.

This is where time slides open
on a sheet of sky, as the churned bodies
of trunks rise for ever, bare
a gleam of white shoulders.

Below the barrier
circles widen, drift eastwards
like green footprints.

Knot

Let me do to you what they do
to the dead – now, while you are still
alive, your blank moon face hanging
half-empty, as if begging.

Let me wash and fill you
with soft white stuff, feed cotton
into your loose cheeks, gather
your jaw shut with silk chiffon.

Let me do it to you now,
paint my cosmetic sunset
across your cheekbones, comfort
your tired eyelids with pennies.

Later, when you die, we can
cut through silk, let the face fly
open, the scarf shake out
its map of escaping creases, as we

roll wet swabs between us
like picnic eggs, the familiar
bag flapping, the small change
jingling again in our purses.

After the Tornado

We have entered your own country
of disasters. The candlelight
gives us all death's-heads, yellow

as ripe cheeses. We eat and laugh
with the living, but we listen
for the silence of a darkened world

that has stopped breathing. Casually
we catch drips, empty buckets,
mop surfaces. Through the man-sized hole

where roof should be the stars
move in. By the smoky flicker
I fill our five plates, pour wine, we even

clink glasses. At last I see you
smile. You are king here. Our dust
settles on your thin crown like kisses.

Midas

You touch grass with your fingertip
and it goes grey, the sky is weighted.
Trees turn to metal as you
breathe on them, the small birds
dropping from their branches
like dull ornaments. My mother's clock
has stopped. A warm mouthful
hardens to lead in your gullet.
Your limbs' own inertia
drags you from the step, your stick
a stiff snake dead under your knuckles.

This is what you wished for, this
has been granted. Your precious daughter
is starting to resemble you.
The whole world swings out
and comes to rest
taut and true as a plumb-line
from your extended finger.

Hans Andersen Plays with Shadows

He might almost have created this
himself, with patience and small scissors:
the split trunk of an old cedar,
twigs spilling in a black fountain.

He could surely have snipped out
these squirrels, their dark bush-tails spreading
in mid-leap, the bunch and stretch of muscle
translated to flatness, shapes pressed on sunset.

His sharp hand might even have added
a corpse hanging from the lower branches,
its twin delicately unfolding
in a crinkle of serrated edges –

enough to make him start shaking
with fear for his intricate creation,
in this world of red-hot skies and bodies
cut loose, worming, so much burnt paper.

My Father Is Shrinking

When we last hugged each other
in the garage,
our two heads were level.
Over his shoulder I could see
potato-sacks.

Another season
and in the dusty sunlight
I shall gather him to me,
smooth his collar,
bend to listen
for his precious breathing.

When he reaches
to my waist,
I shall no longer
detach his small hands
from my skirt,
escape his shrill voice
in the dawn garden.

When he comes to my knees,
I shall pick him up and rock him,
rub my face on the white
stubble of his cheek,
see his silver skull
gleam up at me
through thin combings.

My Father's Handkerchiefs

In a controlled explosion
of dry grief, fragile as skeletons,
trembling in my hand like my daughter's
origami monsters, their worn muslin
stiff with mucus, they let me prise them
open. With a sound like tearing
the crumbs of snot flick out at me,
my father's latest creations
dead. Each week I wash them,
press warmth into the yielding creases
and bring them back – so many
neat flat squares for him
to snort his thick grief into. Each week
I find them again, wreckage
of crippled beasts and flowers
to flutter or creep or scuttle
into my machine
as I try to name them: butterfly,
tortoise, crane, crab, lily,
cygnet, crane, crane, crane, crane.

Forgotten Light

Today I shall draw back the curtain
on the landing, and see lichen
like mustard on the garage roof, the winter
jasmine in the next garden, a year's clouds
blowing in across the ridge-tiles.
My father's pale green carpet
will be as it once was, before shade
turned it to moss. A drift of hand-prints
will rise on the hall plaster
where he has leaned his weight
all these months, the whorls of his grey fingers
like a sleepy child's in the half-dark. I shall
press my own hands in them,
see how our two spans almost
fit, but not quite. I shall see insects
dance on the warm glass, newly woken.

My Father's Caul

Is this my father's skin
or my grandmother's,
twice folded
in its blue envelope,
like a promise of wings?

I tease it open,
see the intimate creases
whitened and flaking,
see my own fingers
shine through it,
as if my father
floated clear of us,
his skin perfect
and impermeable,
his life melting to wax.

Now this dry moon rises
in cold currents.
The attic shadows
play over it.
I see it falling
through air,
its stretch of membrane
slick with grease,
the purple features
flattened to a gasp,
the new-born
mouth, nose, eyes, fingers
sealed in a bag of skin
and sent back to her,
slippery, anonymous.

Protected Species

My parents' papers lie round me
bundled in boxes, the lids dotted
with the droppings of bats, the names
faded, too faint for a stranger's eye
to interpret. I pull, and the perished bands
snap into dust, a grey sheet blisters
with flying fragments. *Joy darling:*
in the roof his circling voice
transmits its high-pitched signal
to her voice. My parents' wartime letters,
starred with small explosions, have flown
great distances, their words blanching
on the page, their steady messages
bringing the world back
to an attic where protected species
hang upside-down, flexing
their claws in a dream of darkness,
shaking their skinny wings.

Talisman

Tonight I shall let the train take me
in a long clanking dream of America,
freight shifted from coast to coast,
dark wagons scratched with symbols.

They will carry me to my father
in his country. Dark-suited, in a trilby,
he leans through steam to wave to me,
his furled newspaper brushing the window

while at the far point of the garden
the child stands watching, goldenrod
bursting on her head as the red spiders
blister the fence like rust, where

adders lie sleeping. This is her penny,
thin as a new leaf, its veins
beaten in bright metal, where the wheels bit,
his old face gone, clean now as a whistle.

The Clever Daughter

(after a misericord in Worcester Cathedral)

For six hundred years I have travelled
to meet my father. *Neither walking nor riding,*
I have carried your heartbeat to him
carefully, to the sound of singing,
my right hand growing to horn.

Your head droops in a stain of windows
as we come closer. The man who made us –
hare and girl – will barely recognise
the lines his blade left: six centuries
have fused us to a single figure.

Clothed and unclothed, we shall reach him,
netted at his cold feet. But as he unwraps us,
my cloak-threads snagging and breaking,
I shall release you, your pent flutter
of madness. And we shall see you

run from his hands and vanish,
your new zigzag opening the cornfield
like the path of lovers, the endless journey
shaken from your long ears, my gift to him
given and yet not given.

Soar Mill Cove

For now the sand holds
the print of feet: an old film
whirrs in slow motion

without burning. These boys
are any small boys, on tiptoe
across shingle, their shoulders

jutting like wings. Settled
behind wind-breaks, our mothers
click their squares of short needles,

re-footing last year's socks; the father
stands with his camera to catch
a son's grin, his perfunctory

peck on barnacled rock,
the girl recoiling. Now they will
kiss until the film melts. Watch

how they repeat us,
how we start to shine, backlit,
as we drop from the frame like stitches.

Burgh Island, 1st September

I could stand here all night watching
the tide come in, where unknown children
squeal as the sea wraps them
in cold, and the next wave crawls towards us,
wriggles into footprints. I could
begin to admire God,
His repeats and ritual hesitations,
the lace of brown scum His slow fingers
have ravelled, His sliced shells and pebbles
in subtle calibrations as the sea stirs them
and leaves them, a moated castle
levelled to a streak. All night I could stand holding
the straps of my flapping sandals
till the land was a cold stroke in darkness
and the strait opened to my bare feet
in running furrows, the one causeway
narrowed to a spine of ripples
and the Island, its hotel, its sharp grasses,
cut off – till the sea tractor
lumbered out again to its harvest of water.

Starehole Bay Sphinx

I stare at rocks and see
no answer, the old paws
clenched on spray, the haunches
furred with bracken, tawny gorse.
As if blown here,
this desert creature crouches,
the head severed,
knuckles still clutching
at low water, the body
discrete and predatory. I will not
tell it what I know, I will not
throw down the mauled syllable.
It waits. The one eye
opens on air. A cloud
floats up like an iris. Below us
the waves break, gleam, whisper
What animal, what animal?

Jocasta's Gift

Let me tell you what I have saved for you:
my wise hands, the years of whispers,
an old shadow rippling across desert,
the cave-mouth echoing with jackals.

Your scarred footprints lie drying on marble
as dawn washes the standing columns.
You sleep perfectly at my dark nipple,
my strong scarf twisted, heavy with water.

It was a good storm, it is a very clean city
in the rags of its surviving palm trees.
The ruins begin to outlive us.

But I have saved you your mother's body,
her red brooch dripping into darkness,
the night voices of all our waking children.

Device

Rampant on red, stark as a small scarecrow
on a ground of sunsets,
it spreads its two limbs

in warning. Far off, in the deep furrows
the life still ripens, bursts, bleeds
to nothing as the inner weather

still changes, washes
the outstretched arms in a sudden flood
of colour. It is evening. Now the horizons

are fading. The silver flocks
rise up and up. A last gleam
plays on copper like September lightning.

Three Tales

(after Flaubert)

I

You are the butcher saint: the mouse
bleeding on cold stone, the sleepy
birds chopped from branches
still ring you with longing – the stag,
the fawn slaughtered with the mother.
No wonder your own parents
lay in your marriage-bed, as if resting
from unnatural acts, no wonder the stranger
called you from across the river
to ferry him in death's own weather,
then wrapped you with his old man's body,
his sores embroidering you like cloth, your skin
clothing him, your hermit's hovel
split from ear to ear, your poor roof
flying wide open, as you
became stained glass.

2

She is the consummate dancer,
her grey silk shadow on marble
as her scorpion body arches
its fountain of piercing juices.
From the floor she can almost see it,
the grey-faced prophet's sneer
from the pit, the hungry trophy
hauled between them for centuries
across desert, crying its dead message.

Before them she still dances; she knows
she is beautiful, that heaven
and Herod jump to her rhythms,
her bent spine, her eyebrows black
as wingtips; and she dances
for the ruler with his poor hunger,
for the glutton puking under the table,
for her mother, for her life; and she pictures
a man's head on a platter – what else
should she ask for?

3

Here is the makeshift altar
set up in a back courtyard,
her flowers and jumbled objects,
her glassy moth-eaten treasure
and these its loveliest feathers,
that patch of surviving wing-silk
like sky spread there under her,
loud with the pulsing heat-haze
as she dies –
blue as unmapped countries,
beady with bright languages,
screeching the mimic diction
of the Holy Ghost,
settling on her shoulder and clawing
at her nightgown
like a lover, a lost child,
her own heart.

Monet: The Chicago Haystacks

It has taken us years to create
this palimpsest: haystacks pregnant with light,
these shadow-skirts belling
towards onlookers. Now we have surrendered
our coats, our back-packs, our tweed
headgear. Our necks no longer remember
zips, the snap collars of down jackets:
now there is nothing between us
but a plastic chip. Your fruit-shimmer
becomes our breathing, your snow
melts for us; your sharp stalks
write on our cold faces. In layers of light
the mottled stack reclothes itself.
Our eyes blink back ghosts, our fingers close
on air. Leaving our shuttered lenses,
our Walkmans' coiled umbilicals
of flex, our shiny packages, we have reached
into light, snow, haystacks. Our bare hands
rifle you, topple your ricks
with inept strokes, as we roll together
in interior dark. We look at you. We shimmer
with death, rose, winter, peeling you
to see one another.

May Dogwoods

From the matted crannies
of ravines, their wings flutter
in pale flocks, gleam like relics
of frost. Up tangled hillsides,
through the close sweat of valleys,
I follow the trail of flowers
to its end, this intimate meeting
of white on pink, each delicate centre
pinned on clear ether. My path dissolves,
winds into silence, woods settle
over woods, wings on wings –
the high crowns of trees
slow-dance like church-spires.
He comes at me, his tight-knotted
sneakers slung across one shoulder,
close-clipped head gleaming
through dark froth, his skin smooth
as iced coffee, grins,
'Hi.' Light glances,
picks out his roadside shack,
its blue tin roof;
the road we walk on
shimmers like water.
'Hi,' I say. 'Hi. Hi.'

Joy

The authorities do not permit us
to take pictures: this dance is ephemeral
as sex or April dogwoods, the pink-skirted
ripple of her body, her emaciated
trunk gleaming, the snapped wishbone
of her thigh sparking light. The pink wit
of her flexed foot stirs us unaccountably
to laughter. This is the dancer's way, this meeting
of tangent bodies, this cool coffee
at café tables, the momentary pink stasis
of words, the fading blossom
drifted from chestnuts. This must be spring,
her limbs' own joy, as his arms lift her,
carry her on his shoulders
into darkness. We may not take pictures.
We look and look, drinking
the small death of each step, each contact
of flesh on sliding flesh, the precise circles
of what we crave, the gasps that express us.

FROM

OPEN DIAGNOSIS

(1994)

I

Bear Country

This is bear country, forest of eyes
and fur, all the black rainbow
from coal-dust to cinnamon.
Trees bristle, rub themselves
electric in shadow. This
is what dark is. Starlight
turns my hair white as I crouch,
pans gold in my small puddle.
In the tent my sleeping daughter
sniffs, grunts, rolls into dream again
under her borrowed ceiling of canvas,
sees the brown skin of marshmallows
blister in the heart of campfires.

Seeing with Hands

She plays at Helen Keller,
measuring the unfamiliar
rooms, eyes shut, touching
their dark furniture.

She walks stumbling on treasure –
a stamp, a coin, a needle –
crouches with spread fingers,
breathing the floor's honey.

Will she learn the stiff reek
of love on sheets, know the night
rhythms, read the bumps
on recurring faces?

Outside she crumples red-gold
and russet, shreds paper
veins between her fingers,
feels the seed-pods rattle.

We watch her through glass,
distrust our adult senses
to spell out 'water' when
the pump groans and spits silver.

Cutting Your Hair

I follow the soft valley of your
nape, parting the hidden
shafts to the scalp, white and unwrinkled
as the skin of a boy I once saw
shivering on a field, his hair
teased into rosettes like a guinea-pig's.

You lean forwards for me, your back bony
as the body of a boy
crouched on wet sand to hold back
the sliding ramparts, a scummy trickle
veining the sleek water.

With the scissors I make you
new, your bent head
close as a baby's. Standing
to explore it with your man's fingers,
you look down at what I have cut off,
thanking me through a fine rain of needles.

Sleep

Our bedroom that year would hardly
let us sleep. Across the white bedspread
the snow-light would run in rivers
as we tossed to the crack and creak
of hardwood. At 2 a.m. we would surface
to the water-softener's slow rush,
waking us into dark, a displaced morning.
Sometimes from the night bedside
a Midwestern voice would ask us,
'Is Bobby there?' Once, on an afternoon
when white sun fell through the leaves
of the maple and kids cried out
at baseball, the curly flex connected
me to death like an umbilical.

On the wall
by the dry splash of last summer's mosquito
the Georgia O'Keeffe iris was
secret and erectile, its sleep-coloured fissure
rising from vague leaves as if to stand
for the shape of all dreaming.

Voice

In the garden shed, among flower-pots,
his words explode into her:
You fucking cow, you came out here
just to...all you fucking wanted...
As I peg out the laundry
I hear him still haranguing
silence, her answers whispered so low
they could be absence. He pauses
to pant and breathe and she
emerges, head bowed, carrying a teacup.

Later I hear them in their adjacent
bedroom, their old bed-springs
creaking, his spent mouth finally
quiet, as a new voice gurgles and rises
in her throat, calling
like a muezzin or a goatherd,
bridging the strange intervals.

Inheritance

They are the real fliers,
these infants in back-carriers,
Moses baskets: through sun
and mackerel cloud they never wake,
faces squashed into arm-rests
or the hollow of a mother's
shoulder as we travel
back into daylight. Over Seattle
we bank. Sun reels on our ceiling,
and they hang level
in a hammock of warm skirt,
still rock on the home runway.

When lights flicker our final
descent, will they still be
above us, so many blind cherubs rising
and falling, sucking the thin air
like milk? When we hit
will they follow us
more gently, their sleepy
pucker of mouth leaving
soft prints on mountains?

II *Open Diagnosis*

Plates

(to Alison)

When they gave you your plates
to hand on to some new doctor,
you held them up to the window
and saw the sky in them,
the river running through your skull,
twigs meeting at the cerebellum,
your brain uncurling, tentative
as a snail on its late glide-path.
Since then I have often thought
of snails and their reflexes,
seeing a slice of America
green through your head's filter.

Homing

Right in a strange country
was left in some lost cell.
I catch myself on corners
trying to look both ways:
on a stranger's bicycle
I circle endlessly
before I can be sure of leaving
in the appropriate direction.
In my last note home
I wrote 'dady' for 'baby'
and let the rogue letters fly
like a pair of silly pigeons.

When a door against me
says HƧUꟼ, I push.

Vocabulary

These flora and fauna have no names:
crimson-bodied, orange-throated,
black-gold mosaic-winged,
straight-stemmed, shrill-voiced,
they mass in skeins, packs, shoals,
howl through dark or flash silver,
bending, beating, reflected in still water.
Later I learn them from books:
cardinal, Indian paintbrush, coyote –
match each with an image and mount it
in sequence on blank paper: cholinesterase,
multiple sclerosis, poison oak.

To Remember

This is not the *Titanic*
because there are no icebergs
in Lake Michigan in summer
to block out stars from portholes
with a sheer face of darkness,
no deep shudder
from keel to crow's nest, no scrape
of nails on locked doors between decks;
no women or children screaming
audibly; there are life-preservers
forwards at all levels – they told us –
and only a brass quintet
of teachers on vacation
to play us out
to new journeys, absences,
a call between two continents,
as we chew on fried chicken,
pour wine from brown paper.
It was too late then, surely,
to watch a thin sunset
push out from its belly of raincloud.

And besides, we are not 'unsinkable',
and it couldn't have been Bach *they* were playing.

World

This is the world.
Eat it quickly
segment by segment
before it shrivels.

This is the pith
clinging to your fingers
in bitter tatters
every white scrap.

This is the smallest pip,
sclerotic raindrop
full of forgotten
juices. Crack it open.

Imaging

We sat in each other's arms
on the couch to watch *2001*, the white planets
waltzing to Strauss, the weightless
travellers, their breath freezing
on little windows, as we waited
for the one moment when Hal would sing
'Daisy', his mind slipping out in segments,
juicy as a blood-orange.
And we savoured
the rainbow plunge into light,
the eye blinking into focus,
the purple and yellow landscape of destination.

Tight in my time-capsule,
head taped to this strange pillow,
I blink blue and gold,
violet, magenta, as a well-placed mirror
shows me creatures from Jupiter
who move behind glass and measure,
then trundle me into air again,
empty me into a strange century,
my brain imaged on a screen behind me.

I know what they see
of a woman's head, poor world
careening into the dark,
white seeds sleeping under the surface:
they see the future, earth-
landings, slow waltzes, time-travel,
while I still squint and blink
at the gift of so much colour.

Germinal

This is my disaster.
The props were worm-eaten.
The roof fell in predictably.

I smell it coming like water
or fire in dry wheat-stubble,
the rush of air in the lift-shaft.

Pushing into hot earth
with the dust-screen behind me,
I can hear blind horses choking.

The sweat runs, stripes me
black in waves. My face bleeds
the mine's own colours.

At the end of the tunnel
I take out my flask, tear
my wedge of bread into daily pieces.

Here is the place, the perfect
platform, where I huddle,
hallucinating, thirsty for surfaces,

and wait for the warm tide to cover
my feet, my ankles; the intimate
nuzzle of an old lover's body.

Correspondence

(to J.S.)

You told us your mother should have
shot herself at a precise moment
some time after the diagnosis,
letting the bullet carve her head
into space for her growing children.

I catch myself smiling, as I tell you
we don't carry guns in England
and you write, 'Don't worry, it's not time yet,'
lean back in your chair to chuckle.

In our downstrokes I see her,
on sofas, in a vintage wheelchair,
the locked drawer you could never
turn your back on. Funny how
she walks the Atlantic
in both directions,
making us both laugh.

Buying Fish

I am one of you, though you do not
know it. We are all hesitant, we are all
gentle and elderly. Together
we point and stutter. Our string bags wait
for wet parcels, gape to receive
the same slippery gift. Tonight we shall all
search our mouths for bones,
as the fragile skeletons
are picked clean, discarded, wrapped in plastic
to cheat the rough tongues of cats. I am
one of you. Watch me buy a thin fillet
of plaice for my single serving, drop keys, fumble
the change. I can beg as well as you
for a few sprigs of sour parsley. I can look
a whole slab of rainbow
trout straight in the eye.

Strawberry-picking

One day a man came to us
with a small jar, asking permission
to scatter his mother's ashes
in the light that lay like dust
between the rows of Red Gauntlet.

Then we picked strawberries
as if an old woman knelt with us
on that sun-striped hillside,
watching our fat fruit mount
in punnets, eyeing the most luscious,

pouncing on straw, slugs, bird-pecks
our young hands had passed over,
reading weights over our shoulder
till the farmer called out, 'Time,'
and we walked to where the wind couldn't blow her.

A disabled toilet is

wider than for ordinary
women because you would need more
space a sloping polished
rail in case you should suddenly
reach out even the paper dispenser
fuller the shiny black floor
twice the width in case you should suddenly
dance slide pirouette see
a whole line of faces in it
roll about laughing
even the graffiti

scratched at ground level you could
make noises grunt heave
gargle your saliva to a tune from *Carmen*
until ordinary women
got down on their knees to peer under
your locked door at wheels
drawn up to the high pedestal.

Blind Skiers

We shrink at the edge
of the piste to avoid them, the blind
skiers with their fluorescent lettering.
This sheer white space
is theirs to practise survival on,
tilting into emptiness –
our hairpin of imagined traverses.

With a soft crunch
they leave us standing, where we can see
white hills and gullies, sun,
the deeper white of shadows,
our skin burned visibly.

They lean out into the valley
where a sprawl of villages
sleeps already in starlight.
Under their feet the moguls
flex curves of dark muscle.
Black snowflakes melt against their faces.

Re-entry

Rewinding the taped
music I first heard the evening we came down
from Alpe d'Huez, I see winter
change to spring as we lose height,
ferns grow like human hair
after death, unknown flowers
sprout where the black snow ends.
Our double-decker
sways slightly over the impossible
drop, slows at each hairpin, almost
to a standstill, levels like a lost heartbeat –
picks up its laborious zigzag,
another few metres. Leaf-buds
brush the window, burst, twist open
as it unwinds again slowly, this record
of time spent in a cold place –
how we said goodbye to everything –
how we came back to meet the flat fields,
our feet swinging over young larches,
birdsong rising from the valley.

Coming Out

I have always been
this. I have always
had an invisible limp,
a peripheral numbness, always
seen men tower over me,
as if from a wheelchair. I am
already blind, have always
mistaken the necessary places,
never been good enough
at guiding food to my mouth,
finding the exit.
This is what I am. I already
speak as if drunk, stain
my bed each night
as I dream. Now I can say it
quite openly: as I
came out for those last
tests, wiping raindrops
from my high saddle
under blue sky, I could have
smiled, laughed, sung
all the way to the hospital.

Message from Galena

In the blue pool, her body
was like anyone's, flattened as ours were
by refraction, fish-pale, only the water
making it monstrous. She swam
almost as we swam, one leg trailing
imperceptibly, cutting through light
as we all did. In the changing-room,
walking slowly with a stick, she would still
walk almost as we walked, her wet body
glowing, leaving a line of footprints.

In that other pool in Galena,
Illinois, I couldn't watch him
as he lowered himself from his wheelchair
to the steps, his heavy torso waiting
as the water danced, its white ripple
of chain-mail ready to wrap him. I couldn't
watch him, couldn't look at
even the empty chair, the long vista
to the lake, down through bare branches.

And yet I am still swimming
as I have always swum since childhood,
feeling something like seaweed between my toes,
still breathing, combing the cold with my fingers,
as my weed collects other weed,
and trails out behind me,
waving green, dark rust,
hosting barnacles, whelks, winkles, mussels.

When I am blind I shall

paint pictures: take a step backwards,
point my brush like a knife and dare
the canvas to come closer, all my creations –
fruit, flowers, fields, clouds,
nudes – stippled all over
with wet sunlight pungent as leaves,
as I touch here, and here, and here, as we used to
pin tails on donkeys.

When I am blind I shall not

write in colours. As I come down
over the headland, the bay's silver
surprises me, and the blue mountains,
the white-rimmed clouds, the black
of high fir trees, the road-signs
like mustard. I shall write sun
and shadow by the sweat on me,
hills by my heartbeats, the angle
at my ankles, write this other landscape
by smell, the taste of
salmonberries, hearing the birds
and the wind always, the shriek
of a July firework echoing on a barn,
the beep-beep-beep of something heavy reversing.

On Being Eaten by a Snake

Knowing they are not poisonous,
I kneel on the path to watch it
between poppies, by a crown of nasturtiums,
the grey-stripe body almost half as long
as my own body, the formless black head
rearing, swaying, the wide black lips seeming
to smile at me. And I see
that the head is not a head,
the slit I have seen as mouth
is not a mouth, the frilled black under-lips
not lips, but another creature dying; I see
how the snake's own head is narrow and delicate,
how it slides its mouth up and then back
with love, stretched to this shapelessness
as if with love, the sun stroking
the slug's wet skin as it hangs
in the light, resting, so that even the victim
must surely feel pleasure, the dark ripple
of neck that is not neck lovely
as the slug is sucked backwards
to the belly that is not belly, the head
that is merely head
shrinking to nameable proportions.

III

First Poem

They found their first country, found
gardens, a white landscape, snow-covered, no
mother. Their widowed father
must have created it, their two soft bodies
purple with frost, mottled, the tree
strung with ice, the brittle apple
glass-coated. As he bit into it
it splintered. When she held it
she left her own finger
stuck to the dark surface
to fall and be buried
by blizzard. And he remembered
how God had peeled back
the skin over ribs, how they had shivered
uncontrollably, gone almost mad
with cold as she had met him, their teeth
rattling, tongues like sucked icicles. Leaving
the footprints, the core, her small finger
still clinging, they knew only
a thousand words for snow: the fur
leaves that would cover their crotches
were very welcome.

The Laughter of Dentists

Since there is so much laughter
in dentists, it was hardly surprising
to hear how that master-craftsman
of amalgams and crowns and bridges
had removed his long white rubber
gloves for his dental-nurse mistress,
how they sat in his surgery together
each night after the last departure
and breathed gas, undressing each other,
laughing uncontrollably at cavities,
haunted by high-speed screaming,
chipped enamel, abscesses, root-fillings,
the stretched mouth of pain under them,
that could rise at the touch of a button.

Hitler and His Mother

À l'heure où je vous parle, Hitler s'est endormi
en suçant son pouce...

PATRICK MODIANO,
La Ronde de Nuit

Did even Hitler have a mother
to feed him and wrap him in towels,
lower him to the rusty water,
while above him the geyser
snorted its hot message? Did he lie there
and splash gently, bending his fat knees,
squealing as she sponged suds over him
like another skin, soaped him
in the folds of his chin like a baby?
Did he look up at the ceiling,
follow the old cracks running
from one corner, forking towards sounder
plaster? Did he see spiders? When she
lifted him and folded him to her
did she play counting-games with him –
church, steeple, clergyman,
little piggies – call him
the cleanest one in the family,
show him his white skin all wrinkled
as the water ran off him in rivers,
dance like a child with him,
tell him he had washerwoman's fingers?

Hamilcar's Daughter

(after Flaubert)

It is about a girl standing on a staircase
hung with figureheads. It is about gardens,
the slow sunset over terraces.

It is about a slave's speeches,
purple, ivory, gold, spices; about weeping
skin, the oiled Suffete in his close litter.

It is about entry through echoing channels
to the secret, fur-carpeted passages
alive with sparks, the reptile's

cold slither between chained ankles.
It is about the unthinkable
veil of the Goddess, a river

rusty with corpses,
the torn ears of elephants, a parched
city besieged by black skeletons.

It is the death-prayer in the young girl's
curtained alcove. It is the high panic
of a pack of skittering monkeys

with familiar faces. It is history. It is
palaces, pits, pavilions, mercenaries,
eaters of unnamed delicacies.

It was the pattern of shells at the threshold,
her holy fish massacred in the fountain.

First Coming

She might have been sleeping on a flat roof
or making bread, or pounding the wet linen,
her back turned to Him in an arched doorway,
or singing as she walked home carrying water.

There was no time to wonder if she knew Him,
if He was the father of someone close to her,
no time to gasp, or cry out – before He was on her
like a robber, pinning her wrists and burning

His precious liquid into her
like acid or molten metal or the swarming points
of hot starlight. She bit down
on His tongue, and found her mouth full of

nothing, she pushed at Him
with all her frantic fingers, and met
no resistance as her body let down its mane of bright
blood, rasped by a swollen emptiness.

What she heard
was her own voice, her own breathing
as He etched His need into her, and withdrew,
the dry streams still criss-crossing her like a delta.

Now she can sing
her magnificat – sing it each morning
as she bends over the cool basins,
her hair sticking to her cheeks, her new body

shaking as if it did not belong to her.

The Ark Speaks

As I lay open, you animals
entered me, male and female,
the slavering bull with the ring
came into me, and the cow, the dog,
the sleek bitch; the twin swan-necks
stroked my bare ribs to a gleam
of feathers. Your hooves,
cloven and uncloven, in a cacophony
of echoes; your slow
paws padded across me,
your ingenious beaks
pecked at loose splinters.
In distant passages, what lashing
scales, what scratches,
what lurching victory
of fur, your exotic couplings! You
requisitioned me, crusted my hull
with droppings as I rang
to your screeches. The roaches
swarmed in me, your foul straw mounted
in a steaming bounty
of trapped gases: male and female
lay twitching. And the waters receded
like sleep, my keel nested in branches.
A door creaked, a hand opened. Like an arrow
the raven flew straight out of me.

FROM

SINGING UNDERWATER

(1992)

After Sixteen Years

You sprawl from the bed
to the floor, a sweet ache
of space between limbs, no
words. I curl, sniffing you,
feel the brush of strange hair
against my knees. Pictures
are thrown up on screens:
our old wallpaper, a milk-float
in a lane, a woman
buying pastries, a tree.
You see gangsters, islands,
black satin, chalk-dust. I
comfort the tip of your lost tongue.

Sometimes we still do it
in our sleep.

On an Error in Your Passport

You were born unexpectedly
exactly a year too early,
making us parents while we slept.

He and I need not have known
each other. You were unwanted,
unthought of, unscanned,

unprepared for. A day and night
of panic was all we had.
I lay shaking on a bed.

You were our first emergency.
The screen across my belly
seemed makeshift. I cried

Do it, oh do it. From the dark,
raking with cold fingers,
they lifted you free

and dangled you high over
me like a garden carrot,
your long head orange as if in sun –

and he, by a fluke of timing
not there, not having come.

Four months later the sickness began.

Singing Underwater

(to my daughter on her birthday)

Together we go down,
knees bent to our chins,
hands fanning the water.
We crouch on the bottom
shivered with reflections,
where thrashing limbs live,
and white-boned feet.
Your hair escapes outwards,
teased by sudden currents.
Your gold eyeballs protrude.
You tug on me and gesture,
mouth opening and closing,
wrapping me in new water
from my crown to my cold toes.
In a rush of blind bubbles
your underwater raspberry
bursts the surface with a roar.
But underneath, the thin tone
of the newborn, lamb, kitten,
or monster. Happy Birthday.
I recognise your tune.

It is not difficult,
the repertoire of the fishes.
You rise with me from three feet
of water, and you splutter.

Nose-bleed

White figure hunched on the stairs,
you breathe blood into clenched fingers,
dyeing handkerchief, carpet, pillow,
bedspread: small animal shot
on snow. You blink and shiver,
pinch back the rich stream
as they taught you. Gently
I wipe blood-crust from furrows,
hold my own breath, counting.

Now the whites lie soaking
in salt; the bed is stripped.
On my knees I track blood spots,
rubbing at your dark coinage
to make this stubborn floor shine.

Voices

My mother's voice, long-distance,
is thin, the silence of sea-beds
in it, darkness, the weight of water.
From a room upstairs my sick child
calls, and I go to her: high
shapes of wind-lifted branches
ripple across her bedspread.
This one I can comfort, her body
plump as grapes, her light hair
breathable: read her the old stories
in a gamut of assumed voices. All day
I run up and down the bare treads,
listen for signals, for a long space
of silence, carry messages or snacks
or empty plates in both directions.

Snow Monkeys

We saw a programme about snow monkeys
and marvelled at how the old mother,
paralysed below the waist, still cared
for her children, how through the winter
she still dragged herself and slithered
in a clot of snow to a lip of summer
by hot springs; how she went on
to have more children as her daughters
matured around her, still groomed them
with stiff fingers, snowflakes in her
beard, the folds of skin still hanging
from her eyes intelligently.

Mermaid

My daughter lies in her bath,
a mermaid in two inches.
As the water slurps and gurgles,
she giggles, sealed tight
into her tail, half-beached,
small fronds of pubic hair
combed parallel like so much
emerald weed.

Shall I go now, shall I
leave her to her two inches
of ripples, long legs
forming like a woman's,
scallop of breasts, wet hair
flopping? But she slaps
her fish-tail on the bottom
and still wants me.

One day soon she will
demand a closed bathroom,
soaping her woman's body
in silence, or quietly singing
and not call me
when she stands to step over
the side of the bath gracefully
as a dancer taking a knife-edge.

Amish Friendship Bread

Day one: do nothing. Accept
what has been given
in a blue and white bowl.

Day two: stir. Bubbles
rise to the surface. The morning
is cool, the window open.
A sparrow scatters drops from
wings dipped in my birdbath.

Day three: stir.
The mixture smells yeasty,
foams like a new planet.
My spoon turns and turns it,
folds it on itself in live
furrows. The sun moves. Children
call across from treehouses.

Day four: stir. It is
puffed and pale as a face.
My spoon punctures it
with sighs. To the east
clouds funnel the darkness,
tornadoes level barns,
trees whip the air smooth again.

Day five: add milk,
measured in a cup. Add flour
and sugar. In its bowl
the batter seethes, crusting
to unexpected proportions.
My daughters, home from school,
crash the house door open,
throw down their backpacks,
catch me heady at the last scraping.

Day six: now there is more
surface for the spoon's wake
to disappear in, a wider

noose of stirring. Through mist
I hear the long flat hoot
of a goods train at a crossing.
Later, sun streaks my knuckles.

Day seven: it swells again,
leaves a sticky tide-mark on
Pyrex. At midnight
I turn off the strip-light
and think I still see it,
the pale rise of moon-cheeks,
twin nostrils black as holes,
I stand at the screen-door
listening for the cry of owls.

Day eight: as I pass through
I write my name with a knife blade.
The reek of yeast
follows me upstairs,
outside, clings to me, heavy
as a child swinging from my neck.

Day nine: I have beaten it
more than once. Now you and I
lie bloated as two babies.
My knees curl in to your belly,
your mouth still drags at the nipple.
Words cream in us as the house
cracks to our combined breathing.

From the hot kitchen
the smell reaches me. I stretch
myself in sun, turn, close my eyes,
my hungry children inoffensive as bees.
Day ten: the bread is ready.

Give
a cup of the culture
to each of three friends,
or to your daughters,
in a small container.

Tell them this is day one.

Ha Ha Bonk

Love the Big Bad joke for adults,
electric custard, gooseberry in a lift.
Why couldn't he have come up with something better?
Knock, knock, I got tired of asking.
Irish stew in the Name of the Law.

And why did the Burglar saw the legs off his bed?
So we could hear the springs creak more clearly?
I wanted to lie low too. Very low, lying with you.
Lying all the time if I could.
Was it that I had stolen something?

And now it goes Ha ha bonk
all down the passage.
A Man laughing his head off.
If I see it rolling I shall pick it up,
carry its belly-laugh with me on a silver plate.

Head-lice

They told me, always keep a bottle,
labelled, on the top shelf,
for the unwelcome discovery.
Then one day I found them,
pearls in the undergrowth.
I could have held them in my hand.
But murder is a modest little need
you can prepare for, like love,
or contraception of various descriptions.

Moderato

(after Marguerite Duras)

My child never played the piano.
It was the clarinet mostly.
You can't count a recorder.
And no escaping boat crossed the window
from frame to horizon.
She played in a pink-gold room under the lamp,
and the flowered curtains remained closed.

There was no murder in a French café.
No crowd gathered.
Our crimes were quite bloodless.
No one was escorted to the closed van,
desire still smeared on their faces.
For us it took somewhat longer than a week.

But there was a magnolia tree, certainly.
The smell of flowers was all down the hill.
I didn't actually press them to my bosom.
My bosom isn't of that sort.
But I did have one in my pocket for a while,
pink and white with brown edges.
And if you had offered me a knife
I'd have slit my throat gladly,
and you might have tried dipping your fastidious
prick briefly in the hole.

Poacher

He seemed almost to like animals.
He stroked their muzzles sometimes.
He was a kind man.
And he gave them no promises:
when the trap's teeth snapped shut,
their own light feet had triggered the spring.

There was no dishonesty in that, surely?
He wore a dark jersey in the dark,
only his hands white in the moonlight.
He did what he had come for.
What did you expect to run into,
stretched low as a shadow under the black trees?

And his bag was there to receive you
merely for discretion's sake along the moonlit path.
He only did what they all do,
except that he would use his voice sometimes
to coax the wildest ones forwards
on to the wire with a soft laugh.

Snap

It was an amateurish angle
for a photograph, heavy trees
reaching, spire's silver needle,
wet grass falling away
beyond a paling. But there was also
the dark, and I had no camera.

Still, I took a snap of your wrist
by feel, my fingers crawling
across dry skin to take
a sliver of flesh in moonlight,
handless, armless – a section
just thick enough for an expert
to tell which way the hairs grew.

Out of the Zoo

We exchanged words
as people do who meet
in anonymous places,
the netting overhead
starred with trapped peanuts.

As you got up to go
a mouse ran out
of the folds of your trousers,
let itself be caught, its frantic
fear-pulse slowed in my bed of fingers
till it lay curled and quiet.

As you opened the door
lice pattered on the pages of my book.
I wrapped them in pocket-fluff,
put them to sleep in the darkness
between my breasts, to fuse
and spread there like milk-drops.

When you left the train
there was a worm on the seat,
wrinkled as an old nametape.
I wound him in a skein,
and made him a nest
in the soft tissue
under my tongue.

Your bland voice however
refuses to be captured.

Anonymous

Six days it took me to do it,
the sweat running off my fingers,
every copy a new masterpiece,
reshaping your smooth world.
I made them all, collage of paper
clippings trembling on the carpet
like coiled moons,
gum worming its necklace,
the mother-segments of sliced sounds.

They were their own sentences,
cut and pasted together,
delighting the fraud squad
who visited you on the seventh day.

Second Coming

You came to us in two colours,
hair and coat streaming,
your lips pursed on echoes.
Your offer was unrepeatable.

You did as we asked you,
gold instrument glinting:
you rid us of our children,
piped them away cleanly.

The last time I saw them
they crouched in the cave-mouth
in a glow of yellow half-life
washed by a dark flood.

Now a grey tide surrounds us,
crush of snouts and bellies
coursing in buried conduits,
succulent as fat fish.

Will you come and take them,
pipe us free of vermin,
our parti-coloured Saviour,
god in two parts?

We sit in our closed houses,
tight and childless as children,
waiting for your second coming,
guarding our precious rats.

Swing-bin

Furled white plastic,
last limp flag on a roll,
this bin-liner (swing, not pedal)
was painlessly separated
along the perforations provided.

Its sides swell now with peelings.
Tea-bags wilt into crannies.
Crumbs of seed-cake dust
the surface with stale pollen
(my mother's tested recipe).

A roll-on deodorant
nudges old rags aside; torn
envelopes, a twist of string
(the kind my father used
to make us kites as children).

Litter of garlic-husk
confetti (to please my husband
once a week on Fridays);
your tapes: rich swill of
Beethoven, Monteverdi,
Katja Kabanova; spaghetti maggots
slide with the subterranean
tremor of springing leaves.

Riding

This is the way the gentleman rides
the lady, trit-trot between unwrinkled sheet
of sky and the earth's soft mattress,
neat as for a gymkhana, dressage kisses
displayed on her sleek forehead.

The farmer studying the fallow
clouds one lost season, slowly
explores his valley of flattened corn.
Clip-clop, blind rider crossing the twilight
bridges, he feels his way home.

But the old man has it, his body
splayed on the ditch-bank, pumping like a
frog's, mouth slippery with leaves,
knobbed fingers still clawing at
contours. You shriek with laughter
at a face seen from underneath.
Hobble-dee, hobble-dee.

Forgetting Hallsands

*(After dredging work connected with the building of Plymouth harbour,
the village of Hallsands was finally washed away by storms in 1917.
Only one old woman remained.)*

It might have been early morning, it might have been evening
when she first saw the dredgers at work out in the bay.
Perhaps the ledge of shingle shifted slightly, polished
pebbles turning to gold on that ordinary day.

She listened for signs, sensing the sea-bed crumble,
measuring time and tide-span against her hand,
but the echoes died in circles, criss-crossing,
and old waves crashed home on the old sand.

Was it a year later, was it much longer,
that the earth sank where the women used to walk?
Half the houses combed away, and half still standing,
scabby with seaweed, bladders drying on the dry stalk.

There were marks on the walls of buildings, warning the living;
where the shingle had reached the stones were black.
She felt the land fall, and the day turned over,
swirling at her heels, glinting, and sucked back.

It was in spring, that equinox, or was it October? –
house after house cleaned on its stone slab,
words torn from mouths in the storm's doorway,
the corner cottage lifted, lurching like a crab.

There were two storms, surely, to crack the village open,
brittle bodies powdered for the sea's bones.
She still hears, turning it over and over,
one freak tide smoothing its bed of stones.

Now, tripping on ruins, plagued by the harsh breathing
of rocks in water, shingle under the rain,
she stops to take shelter in the wells of chimneys,
scanning the dark circle for a belated sign.

Infants

The day thou gavest
with what shall I mend it
there are holes in the roof now
to let out the singing

fragments of broken slate
now the day is over
jelly on the wibble-wobble
milk bent straws in the crate

tippity-tappity on my shoulder
smoke-stains under the eaves
they done it them two together
cowardy cry ouch custard cry

before the huntsman shoots me dead
I never I honestly never I never
windows open to the old voices
steel across the sky.

Sea-anemone

Dark bud, swollen and shining
in the long blink of the tide,
you guard your salt cavern,
sucked bare in your crack of dark weed.

You are closed now. Closed, you glisten,
fat pupil ringed with ripples.
They poke at you with driftwood,
and you are inscrutable as a cyclops.

You sit smugly under the rock
and wait for evening,
fattening yourself on silence,
gorged with sea-creatures.

You are nothing but a blind thing,
a shape, a shell, a polished stone.
A pointed stick could smash you
to a smear of moisture burnt in the sun.

But the tide will find you
with a head-dress of live serpents,
stinging the world to sleep,
licking and leaping when the eyes have gone.

Eve at Autun

You let them in once, the rabble
of pilgrims, craning their necks
to see stone devils, monsters,
wise men like wise monkeys
carrying stone in caskets.
Now they enter freely, no longer need
to took up to count the grapes
chiselled in clusters. Here are the
Child's legs dangling from the donkey,
here is St Joseph in his corner; almost
at eye level Judas chokes on his tongue.
This near space was an arm, a nose,
a finger. No scaffolding.
Ordinary stairs can lead to such places.
You lie on your side, thinking,
your stretched girl's body conventionally
decent. Your cheek lengthens in your hand,
the lichen of Paradise growing in your eye-
sockets, as you grope for the
one tree, now leafless,
and the door stands open, unguarded.

Rings

Let me die like an onion,
on a good block board
by a short clean knifing,
new life still at the centre,
a jet of sharp juice in the eye.
Sever me straight
before you tease me in concentric circles,
dream from dream,
twin from embryonic twinning,
sleep from waking.
Your hand is shaking.
Watch me change my shape
and shimmer under running water
if it makes you cry.

I Am Man-made

I am man-made.
My father made me,
softened and pulled me,
thumbed me full of crescents.

I am man-made.
My teachers made me,
threw and turned me,
textured me with scratches.

I am man-made.
The Devil made me,
moistened and coiled me,
fired me, glazed me
blue-black and green.

Now they are gone,
by whom shall I be seen?

Hall of Mirrors

(to Mara)

In my kettle I have a long head.
My nose swells like a drop
of ripe metal, my chin is melting,
my eyes squash up to the lid.

I have a clutch of white knuckles
smooth as eggs in a steel
saucepan, hair matted with dazzle,
pores big as pin-pricks.

Crouching, I am a child sick
with mumps; as I rise
my puffed jowls puncture, my head
nods over a stainless breastplate.

On tiptoe I am pregnant again
for a moment, silver freak,
queen of the pier-palace,
my skin beaded with real water.

Post Partum

(to Mara)

When you lifted the receiver
I heard crying, my few questions
answered in raucous gasps
of need, bringing it all back –
soapflakes and ammonia,
nape-hair on my closed eyelids,
bars across the window.
I hear the slow creak
of wheels as I walked my daughter,
feet flapping on brick pavements
under rain, the sudden crunch
of a pothole, my own teeth
chattering. You tell me Wait
and there is a new silence
more urgent than my questions,
your mouth drooping as you unbutton
parts of yourself I can imagine.

Black and White

Old Russian woman,
arms like exposed roots,
mouth one level line of shadow,
she stands,
not noticing the petals,
not noticing the clouds,
outstaring the camera,
blossom-drift over her,
freak snowstorm in lush grass,
May-winter.

Because she is old and in black
the May-blizzard shows up on her,
freckled and full of birth as an egg.

Hugo's Long-sleeved Cardigan

was the book I read my daughter
night after night, her eyes closing
as she sucked on two fingers:
the story of a grandmother
not unlike my own mother
who counted obedient stitches
and came up with something
ill-fitting, good only for monkeys.
I can still see that cardigan
behind bars, smeared with banana,
the hairy hand emerging
from stripes, prehensile thumb
bent backwards, looped back over
trapezes, the head hanging
in confined spaces.
                                        And I wish
there had been no banana,
no stripes, no monkeys'
chatter, no empty dangle
of wool, that the endless sleeves
had ended sooner, defiantly,
or that the child's arms
had inched out on needles
to meet her, a few rows longer.

To You on My Birthday

On this day especially
I think of how you
felt yourself abandoned, waters
breaking in blackness as
frightened (you said) by a
horse in a field, stupidly,
you stumbled and felt me
come in a rush, leaving
you empty
four weeks too early,
being too eager (you said)
for what life had for me.
You'd smile as you told me
how Sister laughed and sat me
in the palm of her hand,
two and a bit bags
(you made it) of sugar
and said, She has everything
a young lady should have,
and you cried. (I think
those were the words exactly.)

Breathing Space

He would always walk me
in dogs' mess and sweet-papers,
or out in the country
between banks of high cow-parsley,
ditches alive with nettles,
until our car in the distance
was a small box of nausea
still closed on my mother
and my skin that was cold and strange
as waxed paper, would suck in colour.
'Big breaths,' and I would breathe
perfectly as he walked me,
facing the oncoming traffic, as if
we travelled, the three of us,
under a tight lid
we could always stop to open,
wherever we were, and walk
away from, breathing deeply.

Branches

I saw my father and mother standing
in a pond, against sunlight on rushes,
my mother's thin arm reaching
from between the small suns of water-lilies,
and saw that a spider
had strung threads from my father's knees
to glitter out over the water;
that their bleached bones had hardened
in the green on green of circles
and the paired blue wings of dragonflies,
the minute dance of egg-laying.
And I was glad
that they still stood there, sun-dry and reaching,
and I was grateful
that no one had needed to bury them,
shut them out of all that light.